EXTRAORDINARY TRAUMA TO EXTRAORDINARY DREAMS

HOW PAIN BECOMES PURPOSE AND SURVIVORS BECOME VISIONARIES

SYMONE FAIRCHILD

WITH CONTRIBUTING AUTHORS

Published by CRE Companies LLC / Cesar R. Espino

Extraordinary Trauma to Extraordinary Dreams / Symone Fairchild with Contributing Authors - 1ST Ed

ISBN: 978-1-960665-38-6 (eBook)
ISBN: 978-1-960665-37-9 (PaperBack)

Dedication

To every soul who survived what should have broken them.

To the dreamers who refused to die in the ashes.

To my son—my greatest reminder that legacy is built through courage.

This book is for you—because your rise was never accidental.

It was Divine.

Table of Contents

Acknowledgment

To the courageous co-authors of *Extraordinary Trauma To Extraordinary Dreams*—you are not simply contributors. You are leaders of a new narrative.

It takes extraordinary strength to revisit the moments that reshaped you. It takes even greater strength to transform those moments into medicine for others. You did not write from victimhood—you wrote from victory. You chose to reclaim your voice, and in doing so, you have permitted others to do the same. You chose transparency over silence, power over shame, and vision over victimhood.

This anthology is proof that trauma does not have the final word. Purpose does. Because of your bravery, someone else will find the strength to rise.

Thank you for trusting me with your stories. Thank you for trusting yourselves enough to rise. The impact of your yes will echo far beyond these pages.

Introduction

There were times on my journey when I felt like what I survived would drown me.

Childhood trauma. Silence. Domestic abuse. Moments that could have broken me if I had allowed them to define me. But somewhere within the fire, I began to understand something powerful—trauma is not the end of the story. It is often the birthplace of vision.

This book was not created from a place of pain alone. It was created from revelation. From the realization that the very experiences that tried to silence us can become the foundation of our strength. That what felt like ashes was actually preparation. That survival is not the destination—thriving is.

The courageous voices within these pages said yes to something greater than fear. They chose to transform memory into meaning, wounds into wisdom, and silence into leadership. And that is extraordinary.

If you are holding this book, I want you to know something: your story is not disqualified because it hurt. Your dreams are not unrealistic because you endured. There is purpose woven into every chapter of your life—even the ones you wish had never happened.

I believe that as you read, you will see yourself differently. Not as someone who was damaged. But as someone who was forged.

You are not here by accident.

You are here because you survived.

And now, it is your time to rise.

~Symone Fairchild

Flossie Njama

CHAPTER ONE

WHEN THE BODY SPEAKS

I am often struck by how differently I now understand resilience. Not as an abstract concept, but as a lived, embodied practice shaped by place, culture, and survival. This understanding did not emerge from theory alone, but from a life that began in a rural village marked by scarcity and was later strengthened through migration, illness, and recovery. Looking back, my early experiences of poverty, displacement, and bodily breakdown serve as critical lenses through which I interpret trauma, healing, and transformation. Today, as a healthier lifestyle ambassador and nurse shaped by decades of service, I have the opportunity to devote my time and knowledge to others. My nursing career has taught me that care is not only clinical, but cultural, relational, and deeply human.

Growing up in the village shaped my understanding of resilience long before I had language for it. Poverty was not a distant idea but a lived reality of unpaved roads, the absence of running water, and limited access to basic resources, defined daily life. I did not own shoes until my early adolescence, and education was viewed as a privilege rather than an expectation. Neither of my parents had a formal education, yet their perseverance modeled survival and strength. I lost my oldest brother in a car accident, and he was not found for over a month. Funeral systems in rural Kenya were disorganized and distant, which deepened the trauma. At the burial, I bit my lower lip until it bled as I stood by the grave. Overcome with grief, I tried to jump in after him, but my family restrained me. I later woke up in a small hospital bed, my lip stitched and throbbing with pain. Within this context, I developed aspirations that extended beyond my immediate environment. I dreamed of improving the lives of my family and my village, and of one day empowering others through the lessons born of scarcity.

The village I grew up in was surrounded by tiny round huts made from scrap wood and dented iron sheets. These structures reflected our socioeconomic reality. We were among the very poor. Our hut was constructed from mud and cow dung, materials that were locally available and culturally familiar. The mud and cow dung were mixed with water to form a thick substance that served as the walls of our home. Thick wooden posts, carefully selected from the forest, were used to anchor the structure and form the frame. We had to select the straightest and strongest pieces, knowing that the hut's stability depended on them.

Once the frame was erected, the thick mixture was spread across it and carefully smoothed by hand. This process required multiple layers, applied repeatedly, to ensure the walls would hold once they dried. Even then, the structure was fragile. Every few months, the weak frame would begin to cave in, requiring repairs. Maintenance was not optional; it was part of survival.

Repairing the hut was always a family project. There was no external help, no professional builders, and no financial resources to replace materials. Instead, we relied on collective labor, resilience, and shared responsibility. The home was not just a physical structure but a symbol of endurance within poverty.

Living in this environment shaped my understanding of scarcity, resilience, and resourcefulness from an early age. It taught me how to work with what was available rather than what was ideal. It also normalized hardship in a way that later influenced how I interpreted trauma. What might be labeled as deprivation in an academic sense was, for us, simply life. Yet, these early experiences quietly built the psychological endurance that would later help me navigate migration, illness, and transformation.

Migration, Displacement, and Stress

I believed that relocating to the United States would be the answer. There is a saying that it takes a village, and in this case, it truly did. With borrowed money, loans, and community fundraising, I was able to make the journey, believing I would one day help my family improve their living conditions. I set off towards what I imagined as a land of opportunity and promise. Instead, I encountered profound cultural and dietary disruptions as I attempted to acclimate to an unfamiliar environment. Culture shock, food shock, and the pressures of survival introduced prolonged periods of stress. I experienced homelessness and chronic sleep deprivation—conditions that gradually took a toll on my body and contributed to the onset of illness.

I had to begin from the very bottom.

Before dreams, before ambition, before even the language to name what I wanted, there was movement. Or rather, the absence of it.

How was I going to make any move?

As I struggled with what felt like a reckless idea, I could hear my mother's voice, soft but unwavering, speaking in *Kikuyu*: "*You can do anything you desire to.*" Her voice still echoes, quiet, steady, almost maternal in its insistence. It arrives when doubt grows loud. Some days were more trying than others.

I did not know how to drive. In my culture, driving was a luxury reserved for the rich. It was never imagined as a skill I would need, let alone one that would one day determine my survival. It was not even a dream. It existed beyond the realm of dreaming. Poor Africans did not drive—let alone own cars. Mobility was reserved for those with financial means. Obviously, money had to be part of the equation to afford something as distant as a vehicle. For us, movement meant walking. Long distances were normalized, and endurance was expected.

On those days, I walked two miles each way along the infrequently used railroad tracks in Salem, New Hampshire, to get to my dishwashing job. I balanced carefully on the rails, avoiding the main roads, aware of how I must have looked to the drivers speeding past me. Their stares followed me. I could feel them slow, then disappear.

I remember thinking: *What kind of country has no pedestrians?*

I felt as though walking itself was illegal, as though my body did not belong in motion unless it was enclosed in metal and glass.

New England winters are known to be brutal, but I did not know that then. The winter of 1993 arrived with a vengeance. The snow fell relentlessly, thick, heavy, and unforgiving. In the village, we had no winters. I didn't even know the meaning of the word until then. Cold was something spoken about, not lived inside.

I had no proper winter coat, no boots, no gloves, built for survival. First, the gloves were kitchen mittens. I laugh about that to this day when I share that part of my trauma. There were no buses on my route. The eight dollars an hour I earned was not enough for a taxi. Every dollar had already been assigned: my share of the studio rent, basic personal items, and what little I could send back to my family. So, I walked, making a walking path with a stick. Each stride required extra energy, and I lifted my cold feet from the snow.

I walked through snow that numbed my feet and silence that magnified my thoughts. Each step became an act of endurance. Each mile taught me something about class, invisibility, and the quiet violence of systems designed without people like me in mind.

Labor, Survival, and Physical Strain

Dishwashing wore my body down in ways I had never experienced before. My hands stayed soaked for hours until they wrinkled like prunes, tender and overworked. My entire body ached constantly, and my back became so sore that at times I struggled to lie flat and rest. Physical exhaustion became part of my daily life, not just an occasional discomfort. This was my first job in the USA.

As I pushed through the pain, my mother's words still echoed in my mind. She always reminded me that perseverance would eventually bring change. Deep down, I believed something would give. I held on to hope, prayer, and the quiet expectation of a miracle, even during the most difficult days.

Adding house cleaning to my work became a necessary step for survival. Dishwashing pay alone was not enough and lacked a financial safety net. Cleaning homes exposed me to environments that were both physically demanding and emotionally challenging. Some homes were manageable, but others were overwhelming. Years later, I learned the term "hoarder's homes," but at the time, I only knew them as extremely disordered spaces that required intense labor.

Some toilets looked as though they had never been cleaned with a brush, and surfaces were layered with long-standing dirt. I had to learn unfamiliar ways to clean quickly. Growing up in the village, we used outdoor pit latrines rather than indoor toilets, so this work required both cultural and practical adaptations.

Migration forced me to relearn basic tasks in a new cultural context. Despite the harsh conditions, the physical pain and emotional strain built resilience. Looking back, I now see that this intense labor was not only about survival, but also an early sign of the accumulated stress my body was carrying. Stress that would later contribute to my illness.

Balancing family, nursing school, and several very strenuous jobs placed immense stress on my body. It became clear that I had to pivot. The 16–18-hour days were never-ending. Slowly, my body was wearing down.

Even as the signs and symptoms quietly appeared, I chose to ignore them. Surely, surviving on 3–4 hours of sleep, often on the couch, was taking its toll. Sleeping on the couch kept me in close proximity to my growing daughter, even in exhaustion, because I was still a mother first. My family back in the village depended on me. I could not tell them that the land of dreams was far harder than they imagined. The sacrifice of keeping the dream alive remained.

The fire announced itself

The day finally came. The day when the questions grew louder than the distractions. Where did I go wrong? And from some distant corridor of my mind, a quieter voice responded, almost defensively: I did everything right. Why me? Where do I go from here?

There were people depending on me. Responsibilities that did not pause for confusion. Expectations that did not yield to uncertainty.

For months, I had not felt like myself. Something was deeply wrong. The genderized pain intensified after the news of my mother's death. She was my hero. Being unable to afford to travel back to the village for her funeral worsened my condition. It broke me.

It began subtly. Small dizzy spells that lasted only seconds. Fleeting enough to dismiss. My shoulders ached, but I told myself it was a strain. I was working two nursing jobs. Fatigue was part of the contract. Weight loss followed, but even that found a convenient explanation. Stress. Long hours. Sacrifice.

I quietly shrugged it all away.

After all, the symptoms didn't linger long enough to demand attention. They were whispers, not screams.

I convinced myself they would disappear. They did

not.

What I know now is that those early symptoms were not inconveniences. They were introductions. The opening notes of a symphony my body had already begun composing. I call it my rainbow now. Just as smoke signals fire, those subtle signs signaled combustion. My life, my body, was about to ignite in ways I had never imagined.

The phone call came on a Friday evening—movie and pizza night.

The only evening I allowed myself to be still. The only night off from the relentless rhythm of two nursing jobs. It was my small participation in what I considered the American lifestyle—work hard, push through, earn rest in fragments.

After one of my long, stressful 12-hour overnight shifts, I stopped at the laboratory on my way home to have my blood work collected.

Nervous and with my heart beating fast, I answered and placed it on speaker. "The lab results are back," the physician said. His voice was measured, but firm. "You need to report to the nearest emergency room."

The room shifted. The air thickened.

There are moments in life when time fractures—when seconds stretch into something unrecognizable. This was one of them. The results were critical. Immediate intervention was necessary.

What followed was not dramatic in appearance. There were no collapsing walls or cinematic crescendos—just sterile lighting, medical terminology, and the steady unraveling of certainty.

That evening marked the beginning of my journey with Sarcoidosis.

Sarcoidosis is an inflammatory condition rooted in

immune dysfunction. The body's defense system, designed to protect, becomes overactive. It responds to unknown triggers by forming granulomas, clusters of immune cells that can accumulate and damage tissue.

In approximately ninety percent of cases, it affects the lungs and lymph nodes. But it does not confine itself there. The skin, eyes, heart, and nervous system may also become sites of inflammation.

Symptoms vary and may include persistent cough, shortness of breath, fatigue, rashes, and fever. Diagnosis often requires imaging, such as chest X-rays or CT scans, followed by biopsy confirmation of non-caseating granulomas.

There is no cure. Treatment typically involves corticosteroids, such as prednisone, to suppress inflammation and slow progression.

That Friday night did not just introduce a diagnosis. It introduced a reckoning. My body had been speaking long before the phone rang. I had simply chosen not to listen. And now, I had no choice but to listen.

It was both listening to and prioritizing my health. Being out of commission had its load of challenges. I had my family here in the US and a larger Kenyan family that depended on me. This was no American dream. My body had let me down. The next seven months were packed with aches and pains, tears, hardly any appetite, hospital admissions, regret, lack of finances, and barely any support. Though a nurse, I was now a patient. My daughter was my closest support. I dreaded the weekly blood tests. Then, bi-weekly, monthly, and whenever the doctor noted a decline that required clarification. I was miserable.

I had seen it on TV and in movies—how friends and family slowly faded away during moments of need.

"Nobody will come for you." I knew that saying far too well. But I told myself that would not be my story. Oh, was I wrong! I fit right into the statistics. There were bad days and not-so-bad days, and I never looked forward to the bad ones. Being the main provider meant I had to figure it out, illness and all. There was no backup plan. It was just me.

I am my mother's child, village-bred through hardship and lack. I knew better than to accept my current reality as permanent. So, I chose to fight. I chose to research, to experiment, and to seek solutions. Village life was still alive in me; it was in my DNA. I was determined to challenge a disease that was said to have no cure. The hospital admission was long and overwhelming. Endless tests, procedures, and a long list of medications followed—many with heavy and frightening side effects. Once discharged, I knew deep within that I needed another way.

Still unwell, I immersed myself in research. I read books on mindset, healing, and simplified living, slowly incorporating healthier daily routines into my life. I revisited my mother's remedies, the wisdom of the village that had raised me. But I did not stop there. I combined those traditional remedies with what I was learning through deep reading and research. I believed that to create extraordinary results, extraordinary moves were necessary. So, I made them. Even with aches and pains and barely any energy, I learned something almost every day and applied it as best my body would allow.

Around month seven, I began to notice subtle changes. My body felt different—stronger, steadier, and more responsive. The monthly lab work that once brought anxiety slowly started to normalize. I had regained five of the twenty pounds I had lost. Even the prominent neck veins were no longer as visible as before. My daily spinach salads and fresh juice played a significant role in boosting my hemoglobin from a dangerously low 7.0 to 12.0.

During that season, I visited an Amish family in search of a farm that mirrored the simplicity of my village roots. They welcomed me with quiet kindness and allowed me to return regularly for fresh produce. Their way of life—grounded, intentional, and close to the land felt deeply familiar to my spirit. It has now been ten years since that first day of my diagnosis. I recall that first day when I drove down a white sand Amish driveway in the quiet countryside of Bowling Green, Missouri, not just searching for food, but for healing.

Life is meant to be lived as it unfolds. No two lives are identical. They may resonate or share similarities, yet each journey remains uniquely its own. My health scare was a deeply personal experience. One that belonged solely to me. As a critical care nurse, I carried extensive medical knowledge. Yet, that knowledge alone could not shield me from a health crisis. It created awareness, but the rest was mine to navigate.

What it presented to me were choices. Those choices refined my grit. And working that grit with unwavering faith led me to what I now call extraordinary trauma to extraordinary dreams. Sarcoidosis, a diagnosis that once felt overwhelmingly scary, was naturally reversed through intentional lifestyle shifts rooted in mindset, nourishment, and daily discipline.

Today, I stand as a best-selling author, sharing my journey of healing and natural reversal so others may find hope within their own battles. Yet the greatest dream I celebrate is becoming a vessel, a voice, and an ambassador of what I have named a Simple Healthier Lifestyle. It is grounded in mindset shifts, mindful food choices, and daily awareness. Small, consistent habits practiced almost on autopilot, gently guiding the body and mind back toward balance, resilience, and restoration.

In the end, what began as extraordinary trauma through illness, migration, and lived hardship evolved into an extraordinary dream—one that taught me that *my body speaks*, transforming my pain into purpose, my survival into service, and my restoration into a lifelong mission to empower others live a simpler, healthier life.

About the Author

Flossie Njama, RN, BSN, is a Critical Care Nurse with 30+ years of experience, Wellness Mentor, Transformational Speaker, bestselling author of *Village Vibes*, and CEO of Simple Life Healthier You LLC. An NLP Master Trainer, she naturally reversed her autoimmune disease. She created the trademarked Flossie's Turmeric Tea™, a cornerstone of her wellness movement, GPS to a Healthier You. A 2025 Ms. Senior Missouri finalist and DAR Community Engagement Award recipient, Flossie has been featured on Fox 2 TV, OWN Your Now Show, Boss Talk LA, and Dr. Smiley Show. Deeply committed to service, she supports orphanage homes in her birth country, Kenya. She empowers audiences through her 3C's framework—Choice, Commitment, and Consistency—for a simpler, healthier lifestyle with purpose.

https://www.simplelifehealthieryou.com

https://www.facebook.com/SimpleLifeHealthierYou?mibextid=LQQJ4d

https://instagram.com/flossienjama

http://linkedin.com/in/flossie-njama-75a0281a4

https://youtube.com/@flossienjama-simplelifehea7613?si=5R5An1rQxXhpuMTK

https://www.facebook.com/flossie.njama.5

KristleAnn "KAS" Sims

CHAPTER TWO

FAITH IN THE FIRE
FINDING GRACE IN THE BREAKING

It was 2005. I remember exactly where I was when I asked God for a divorce.

I was driving to work that morning, gripping the steering wheel, praying for direction, not knowing what else life had in store. My marriage had been abusive—physical, psychological, and verbal. Every day was a battle to protect my spirit and fight for myself and my child. But I knew the Lord would show me the way and would give me the strength I needed to walk away when the time was right.

That day, everything came so quickly. I had just discovered my husband had been unfaithful. God led me to that truth—I knew in my heart that this revelation would give me the courage to leave and not turn back, like I had once before.

"God," I whispered, "show me the way. If I take this step, will You carry me?"

And then the car filled with a voice—not audible like music, but unmistakable, filling every corner of my being:

"Do not worry. All will be OK."

Peace flooded me instantly. Complete, unshakable peace.

That peace didn't come from knowing the future. I didn't know the trials ahead—the hospital, the surgeries, the blood transfusions, or the terminal diagnosis. I was simply acting in faith, seeking direction, and trusting God to guide me through the unknown.

I initiated the divorce proceedings.

Not long after, I was out of town at national educator training with Paul Mitchell when I woke at 2:29 a.m. in excruciating pain. I wouldn't have survived that night alone. If I hadn't roomed with another educator, I would have bled internally and died in my bed. Two of my co-educators rushed me to the hospital.

Later, I found out I was bleeding internally.

The first hospital in Columbus stabilized me as best they could. But the real progress started when I was transferred to Akron General Hospital. I brought a medical digital drive from the previous hospital. Once the doctors reviewed it, the blood transfusions began in earnest—three separate transfusions, three pints each. Nine pints total.

Even before the transfusions began, the doctors

were shocked that I was still alive. They couldn't understand how my body had survived losing so much blood. Even with all their expertise, they had never seen anything like this. That realization set the tone for the gravity of what was ahead. And yet, I felt no fear. I knew God was holding me. I remembered His voice in my car: "Do not worry. All will be OK." That peace didn't depend on what doctors saw—it depended on what I knew God could do.

They waited five days to perform surgery. Though I had to lie there in the hospital receiving blood transfusions and trying to rest, my body was weak, but my spirit was steady. I will never forget after my first blood transfusion how much color I had in my face, and I felt alive. Every day was a careful balance—too weak for surgery, but too much bleeding to ignore. Even then, the doctors didn't know exactly what they would find once they opened me up. Three doctors discussed three surgical approaches and ultimately chose a gastric bypass to save my life. I trusted the doctor's plan, but more importantly, I trusted God's timing. I had so much peace, and I thanked God for giving it to me.

Right before surgery, my mother and her best friend, my Aunt Betty, stood beside my bed, crying.

"Don't worry," I told them. "It will be OK. I'll see you soon."

I later learned that the doctors had already prepared them I might not survive the surgery, that I was very weak, and my body may not be strong enough with all I had endured. The uncertainty was heavy.

But I wasn't living from probability. I was living on a promise.

When I woke up, I learned what had been done: half of my stomach removed, a foot of my intestines gone, and a gastric bypass performed to save my life.

Two and a half weeks later, I was discharged from the hospital—just a day before my son's birthday. Despite everything, I wanted to celebrate with him, so I took him to Chuck E. Cheese. Even though I didn't know what the future would hold, I stayed positive and believed what I was promised. I focused on the small, valued pleasures and embraced life.

At that time, I had already asked for a divorce, but my husband was still living in the house. I slept upstairs while he stayed downstairs. One evening, we were in the living and dining room near the stairs that led down to our bedroom. He started talking about the divorce, unhappy that I was staying strong in my decision. In a frightening moment, he tried to push me down the stairs out of anger.

It was that moment that propelled me to take immediate action, to go to court to seek a Civil Protection Order, ensuring my safety and giving me the space to focus on my recovery.

After leaving court, I received a call on my cell phone from the doctor's office. They said I needed to come in and speak with Dr. Guyton. There was no explanation. Just, "We need you to come in." My sister-in-law and I had planned to go to lunch. When I told her about the call, she immediately said, "We need to call your brother. He needs to meet us at the hospital."

I said, "No. We're still going to lunch as we planned. Whatever they must tell me, they can tell me when we get there. Daniel can meet us there." I wasn't panicking. I wasn't spiraling. I felt steady.

As we were walking toward the restaurant, she turned to me and asked, "What if you must do chemo or radiation? What are you going to do?"

At that time, I worked on stage with Paul Mitchell. My signature look was wearing hats and ties. I laughed and said, "If I must do chemo, I'll just wear a head scarf and keep wearing my hat and tie like I always do."

That was that.

We went to lunch. We talked. We ate. We didn't let it dictate the moment. After lunch, we went to the hospital and met my brother, Daniel.

Dr. Guyton was very soft-spoken, and you could see he was struggling to share what he had to say with me. He said, "Kristle, we had 5 specialists check your biopsy and reviewed your case. They all came to the same conclusion. There is no easy way to put this to you, but you have spindle cell sarcoma, and from what they could detect, you have had it now for about 2 and 1/2 years. This type of cancer is very rare, and there is no treatment or cure for it."

I said, "OK."

I remember my brother putting his hand on my left shoulder. He said to me, "Kris, did you hear what the doctor said? You're terminally ill."

I said, "YES!"

My brother asked the doctor, "Where do we go from here?"

Dr. Guyton responded, "Kristle, it's very important you do your follow-ups, but I want you to go about your life the same as before you knew you were sick. I want you to keep working. I want you to keep living your life. I want you to stay positive and enjoy your time, but it is very important that you get your affairs in order. You have about a year left."

Even hearing those words come out of the doctor's mouth. I knew I was going to be OK! I was at peace.

Through all of it—the surgery, the bleeding, the

abuse, the divorce—I kept my peace. I lived each day steadfast in the promise from God, trusting His plan even when the path was uncertain. I focused on small steps, one day at a time, holding fast to my faith.

Just like I do day to day now, God continues to fulfill His promises in my life, guiding me toward my purpose. That same faith that carried me through one of the most harrowing seasons of my life is the faith I lean on today, shaping my work, my relationships, and the calling He has placed before me.

During my hospital stay, my head doctor arranged for a nutritionist to meet with me. Now that I had lost half of my stomach and a foot of my intestines, I had to be intentional about every meal—what I ate, how much I ate, and how often—just to maintain my weight and overall health.

Because of the type of surgery I had, I would also have to contend with dumping syndrome, a condition that can cause pain, vomiting, and diarrhea, sometimes all at once or one or two symptoms at a time. There are two forms of dumping syndrome I could experience, and this would be something I would need to manage for the rest of my life.

It was hard to learn what my body would accept and what it would reject at different times. Every meal became an experiment. But I knew something deeper was at work.

Having terminal cancer, going through a divorce, and caring for a young child all at the same time, I knew God was shaping me for more.

The peace I had through it all was remarkable. That peace—the kind that surpasses understanding—can only come from one place. I believed, and I still believe, that source is God my Savior, the Lord Jesus Christ.

I kept up with my day-to-day life, staying positive and happy. I went for my check-ups every three months. Taking the contrast for tests was brutal—my body wanted to reject it, and I had to force myself to keep it down.

One day, I went in for a follow-up with Dr. Remus. It was my third appointment, putting me at the nine-month mark. I had my son with me. He sat on the floor by my side while I sat on the doctor's examining bed.

Dr. Remus was facing away from me. She turned around—not with a greeting, but with an unexpected, sharp command:

"Get the hell out of my office."

I froze, confused. "What?" I asked.

She said, "We can't find your cancer. We can't explain it."

I looked at her and said with certainty, "I can. It's the grace of God."

She laughed. I smiled back. "You can laugh, but I know."

She brushed me off, explaining that she wanted to see me back in six months, maybe a few more times, and eventually possibly once a year. But there was one condition: if my cancer returned, there was literally nothing they could do. No treatment existed for this rare form of spindle cell sarcoma.

She looked confused, but I was not. I knew what God had said to me in the car that day when I was praying: "Do not worry. All will be OK."

Even as I continued working for John Paul Mitchell Systems as a national educator, traveling for hair shows and educating others—work I loved—something inside me began to shift. My career, which had been my pride and passion, began to feel less central. I sensed a calling, something bigger I was meant to do.

Even as I felt God calling me to a greater purpose, I knew that my journey wasn't finished. I felt a deep pull toward law enforcement. I wanted to help people in tangible ways, to serve and protect, to be a voice and shield for those who couldn't defend themselves.

I applied to three large city police departments. Each offered opportunities, but I felt God guiding me specifically to the Cleveland Police Department. At that time, I was not yet considered in remission from my cancer. Cleveland kept checking in with my doctors, concerned about my health and viewing me as a potential liability.

I don't know why, but Dr. Guyton reassured them about me—perhaps it was simply God's plan.

I began the police academy on May 4th, 2009, and was officially sworn in on October 30th, 2009. From the very start, I could see how God's hand had prepared me: every challenge I had endured, every test of faith, had made me resilient and capable of serving others. I was able to help countless people throughout my time in the force, and I knew I was an officer fulfilling what I needed to at that time and learning for what was to come.

But life, as always, has its trials.

On February 9th, 2017, my career as a police officer came to a sudden and traumatic halt. My day began normally, though I wasn't partnered with my regular partner. I started my shift at 3:00 p.m. on a late car, working with another male officer.

At 5:29 p.m., our zone car was struck by two vehicles at an intersection. Other vehicles had stopped around us, obeying our lights and sirens, but one driver did not. That vehicle struck the front push bar of our zone car, swinging us around. Another vehicle followed behind, hitting the rear of the car, and that vehicle fled the scene.

I was the only one injured.

The aftermath was devastating: a severe traumatic brain injury, neck and back injuries, a torn tendon, and a fractured wrist. The TBI brought cognitive struggles, speech issues, panic disorder, mixed anxiety and depression, vision problems, concussive syndrome, and much more.

This was not the first time in my life that I was struck with hardship, but this time it hit differently. I was flat on my back, physically and emotionally, and everything was taken from me: my career, my mind, my verbal speech, and my physical attributes. I was totally dependent on someone else having to physically take care of me, and I felt like a burden. I questioned God. I asked, "Why would You save me from being terminally ill, only to let this happen?" I couldn't understand at that moment, and I was angry. I was angry with God. Not that I didn't love him or that I lost my faith; I just didn't understand. But all of this was for a purpose, and he was going to show me why. There was more for me to learn to get me closer to my life's purpose, and I needed to trust in him. There was so much more I needed to learn about myself, and he was going to get me through it. It took me time and patience, and I eventually came around. I remembered that he had promised, "Do not worry, all will be OK." I just needed to listen, obey, and keep my faith in him and believe.

Even in frustration, I did not lose my faith. I still loved Him. I knew that this, too, was a chapter He had written for me—a lesson, a shaping, a refining process. There were things God wanted me to learn and experiences I needed to face to fully move into my purpose. I had to trust Him, to lean on Him, knowing He would bring me through this just as He had promised.

This was another crucible—another opportunity to deepen my faith, to grow in resilience, and to prepare for the next stage of the life God had planned for me.

Even now, in 2026, I am still dealing with the aftermath of all these events. It has been over 20 years since my battle with stomach cancer, and through it all, I have been a victor through God's grace. From surviving cancer to enduring the physical and emotional challenges of my injuries, to navigating nine years of ongoing struggles with the Cleveland Police Department and Ohio's Workers' Compensation system, the journey has been long and excruciatingly difficult. I officially retired in 2020, but the process of rediscovering who I am continues as I grow. I have come a long way and have learned a lot about myself, and my relationship with God has become even stronger. My faith has carried me where I am today. God has never left my side. Doctors never expected me to be where I am today after my brain injury. I do have a new normal and learn differently. Tasks and skills that once felt natural to me no longer come with ease. Yet I continue to push forward, learning, adapting, and growing stronger every day.

I had to redefine myself beyond the title of "police officer." I am much more than that. These past nine years, though extremely challenging, were necessary. They taught me about resilience, self-discovery, faith, patience, and purpose. I have learned who I truly am, the depth of my faith, and what God has in store for me. I have learned to trust His plan, even when the path is uncertain, and to move confidently toward the purpose

He is calling me to now.

Through cancer, abuse, trauma, injury, and trials, one thing remains constant: my faith in God and His promise, "Do not worry. All will be OK". That peace, which began in a car during a prayer in 2005, has carried me through every storm. And it continues to guide me today, shaping me into the person I was always meant to be.

And I am where I am today—Extraordinary Trauma to Extraordinary Dreams—having cognitive and speech issues, disabilities, chronic pain, and being disabled, to thriving in media, film, and speaking at public events, because God is guiding me to fulfill my life purpose: to help and reach others.

2 Corinthians 5:7 "For we walk by faith, not by sight", (NKJV,ESV)

About the Author

Akron/Cleveland media pro & Diva Locals President, KristleAnn "KAS" Sims, is a medically retired police officer and a strong, God-fearing woman. A stomach cancer victor and a walking miracle many times over. She blends her production expertise with a life of resilience, led by faith and Conviction.

Connect with KristleAnn Sims "KAS":
Instagram: www.instagram.com/kas_sims11
Facebook: https://www.facebook.com/kclilharley
Page: KristleAnn Sims

Jeffrey Sanow

CHAPTER THREE

FROM TRAUMA TO TRIUMPH

The Tragedy.

I come before you humbly with a story to tell, though humility was not what drove me to leave the farm in Ohio. What compelled me instead was a quiet, stubborn refusal to follow the well-worn path laid out for my generation—the 2.3 children, the microwave humming in the kitchen, a refrigerator reliably full, a white picket fence, a mortgaged house, and two cars resting obediently in the driveway. It was the prescribed destination for anyone aspiring to middle-class success in the late twentieth century, and I knew, even then, that it was not meant for me.

I wanted a different course altogether, one that would take me as far from Ohio as possible—and, truth be told, as far from the nation I would later dedicate my life to serving. I did not yet understand that contradiction, only that distance felt necessary. The farther I went, the more clearly I believed I might come to understand myself. The deepest, darkest reaches of Africa seemed like the farthest descent down the rabbit hole I could manage. It was a place untouched by familiarity, beyond comfort, beyond expectation, and exactly where I believed I needed to go. I could not have known then that the road I chose would eventually lead me back, not just to the country I had tried to outrun, but into its service, its shadows, and its moral complexities.

This story begins there—far from home, far from certainty—at the moment I stepped off the path I was supposed to follow and onto one that would define the rest of my life. The painful trauma that ultimately drove me to leave the United States at the age of twenty and live in Africa began long before college, closer to when I was eleven years old. In truth, the fracture started even earlier. Long before I could name it, I knew something was wrong, especially with my mother.

A boy of ten or eleven may not be particularly observant, but we were not blind. Living in relative isolation on a farm, the world we knew was small, and the shouting matches between my mother and father filled it. There was no escape from them—only the raised voices, my mother's drinking, and the whippings that followed. This was the atmosphere of our childhood, and it felt normal only because it was all we knew.

When my parents told my three siblings and me that they were separating and divorcing, it was devastating. At eleven years old, the ground beneath me seemed to collapse. Whatever sense of permanence I believed childhood promised vanished in that moment, replaced by uncertainty and fear I did not yet have the language to describe. A short time later, my mother remarried—to a man she had likely been involved with before the divorce. His wife had taken her own life not long before my parents' marriage ended. Whether those events were connected, I was too young to know and can only speculate. What I did understand was that the adults around me moved forward quickly, while the children were left to absorb the shock in silence.

What I knew was the result: my mother remarried, and overnight, whatever family we had left was blown apart again. I suddenly had six stepsiblings, and any illusion of stability vanished. The chaos didn't stop—it just found a new configuration, one that felt louder, more crowded, and less forgiving. My younger brother and I were then shoved into what passed for normal in those days: every other weekend with our father, holidays chopped up and negotiated like ceasefires in a war we never started. Life became a blur of packed bags, forced smiles, and adults pretending this arrangement was somehow healthy. For us, it was misery defined not by connection, but by constant disruption and emotional whiplash.

About two years later, my father remarried, and four more stepsiblings were added to the wreckage. My stepfather was tolerable. My stepmother, on the other hand, was unhinged—volatile, unpredictable, and cruel in ways that don't show up on family trees or legal documents. She turned an already broken childhood into something chaotic and exhausting, where staying invisible felt like the safest strategy. Each change piled onto the last, feeding a slow-burning anger and a growing need to escape. I didn't yet have a map or a destination, but I knew one thing with absolute clarity: I needed distance—real distance. The urge to leave didn't suddenly appear in adulthood. It was forged here, in the middle of this mess, and it would eventually drive me not just out of the house, but out of the country altogether.

At fourteen, under Ohio law, a child could choose which parent to live with. I wanted more than anything to live with my father. I believed it would mean stability, distance from chaos, and perhaps a fresh start. What I did not yet understand was the reality I was choosing. We do not choose our parents—or our step-parents—but we do choose how we respond to them. At that age, despite the incredible challenges, I was determined to stay positive, to believe that effort and optimism could overcome circumstance. I would soon learn how naïve that belief was.

Midway through eighth grade, I left the farm and moved to the west side of Cleveland to live with my father and stepmother. I was no Cinderella, but the environment was harsh and unforgiving. The epitome of out of the frying pan and into the fire. My place in the household was clearly defined—and it was at the bottom. My "bedroom" was a corner of the basement, wedged beside the washer and dryer, a constant reminder that I was tolerated, not wanted.

My stepmother's hostility toward me was neither subtle nor occasional. It was constant, palpable, and overwhelming. I do not blame my stepsiblings for how I was treated; they were following her lead, absorbing her cues, and learning who mattered and who did not. In that house, I learned how quickly authority can shape cruelty, and how isolation can become routine. By sixteen, the weight of it all had become unbearable. I was deeply depressed and suicidal, carrying more despair than a teenager should ever have to hold. With my father's help, I purchased an Ithaca Model 27 Featherlight twelve-gauge shotgun—a decision that, in hindsight, speaks volumes about how invisible my pain had become. I did not yet have the words to ask for help, only the growing conviction that escape, in one form or another, was the only relief left.

In my senior year of high school, I returned to the farm to live with my mother and stepfather. It was not a great improvement, but it offered something I had been missing for years: clarity of purpose. I understood that staying meant stagnation and leaving—anywhere—meant possibility. That realization alone was enough to push me forward. I finished high school, though not with grades that suggested promise or direction. What I lacked in academic distinction, I made up for in resolve, a resolve that became perseverance and that carried me through all my life. I set my sights on college at The Ohio State University and swore I would never return. With few exceptions, I kept that promise for the rest of my life.

The Triumph.

After two years at Ohio State—a mere two-hour drive from the farm—I came to another uncomfortable realization: I still was not far enough away. Physical distance had become my measure of freedom, and proximity felt like gravity, always threatening to pull me back into a past I was determined to escape. The Peace Corps in Africa seemed about as far from Ohio as it was possible to go. At the very least, it was a beginning.

I would never have started the journey I was about to embark on, essentially running away from home, had it not been for the painful and miserable childhood I endured. It was traumatic and deeply unhappy, and it instilled in me a relentless need for distance—from Ohio, from my family, and from the version of myself shaped by that environment. That impulse was not noble, but it was powerful. It became the cure that drove every major decision I made thereafter and set the course for the life that followed. As a result, my path diverged sharply from that of the average Buckeye. My motivation—escape from my family—is not something I am proud of. Still, the life it propelled me toward is one of triumph.

The lessons learned in that tragedy became a triumph, allowing me to become an international businessman working in a variety of countries, then a CIA Operations Officer for the final part of my career, and to travel to many parts of the world. For obvious reasons, I am not able to discuss the work or exactly where I was. However, as a side benefit of my employment, I was able to visit and delve deeply into different countries, some of which are incredibly significant to our history, culture, and the political, economic, and religious world we live in today.

Imagine walking in the footsteps of St. Paul after he was struck down on the road to Damascus. If you read Acts 9, you will learn of a disciple named Ananias who was instructed in a vision to "Rise and go to the street called Straight and look for a man of Tarsus named Saul." The "street called Straight" still exists. Imagine walking down the same street as St. Paul or visiting St. Paul's chapel or his underground church. Imagine going to St. Paul's chapel in Damascus and lighting a candle. I was able to do that every time I went to Damascus. I am a good Lutheran. We do not generally light candles. That is a Catholic thing, though my pastor does joke that Catholics make the best Lutherans. (Think about it. If you do not get the joke, study the history of the Reformation.) While I have always been churchgoing, I grew in my faith by visiting these sites and seeing the Bible in action. My family and I were able to travel to the Pyramids and the Taj Mahal so many times that our kids complained. "Ahhh, do we have to go see one of the amazing ancient wonders of the world agaaaaaaiiiin!"

The triumph was traveling and working internationally, serving my country, of course, without revealing exactly what type of work I was doing, in places you may not have heard of. Therefore, you have no idea how it impacts your life today. As a businessman, I was always collecting BUSINT – business intelligence.

As I said earlier, I would never have embarked on the journey if I had not had the miserable childhood I did. It was not a good one, and it inspired me to travel as far from Ohio and my family as possible. As a result, my journey is different than your average Buckeye. While my motivation–the escape from my family–is regrettable, I have no regrets for the path I took. In some respects, if I had not had an unpleasant childhood, I may have followed the path of many of my friends and never left Lorain County. What a boring life that would have been.

My greatest hope is to encourage people who have come to a fork in their lives, regardless of the circumstances, and are looking at a different path. While Dr. M. Scott Peck's book *The Road Less Traveled* discusses relationships, there is also the road less traveled to see the world and discover deeper meaning in our lives. I encourage people in their 20s and 30s who want a change of perspective to explore whether there is a path for them. Would a change of scenery benefit your life and help you fulfill your dreams? When I changed my perspective from Ohio State University to North Africa, I had no idea, nor could I have imagined, the path my life would ultimately follow. I will opine that the readers of this may not know either. I hope that this will give you some dreams, just as reading about Dr. Livingston did for me. Maybe it was reading about Sinbad the Sailor. I wanted my life to be an adventure; I did not know how to make that happen. Peace Corps led the way. I also hope that my stories and insights will clarify some of the ways the parts of the world we live in impact each of us today, without our knowledge or understanding. I hope it inspires you to be the change we need. It could change your life; it did mine.

One of the Peace Corps' major areas of focus at the time was rural development and agriculture. There were projects all over Africa staffed by Peace Corps Volunteers and managed by local rural development officials. We were essentially free/cheap labor. Many water well projects were also underway, and my personal favorite was teaching English. The majority of Volunteers working in agriculture and well projects were men. The majority of English teachers were women. Thus, my personal favorite.

Africa was calling, and the Peace Corps was my ticket. I never fully understood why Africa claimed my imagination when Asia and Latin America did not.

Perhaps I had read too many stories of African explorers and adventurers. Perhaps it was my Scottish heritage drawing me toward figures like David Livingstone—the missionary and explorer who survived a lion attack, charted the Zambezi River, and quite literally walked across the African continent. When journalist Henry Morton Stanley famously found him in 1871, it launched a legend. Maybe, on some level, I wanted an adventure of my own.

Years later, that same restlessness resurfaced. A chance advertisement in the *Wall Street Journal* led me to the Central Intelligence Agency, where I could channel my international experience into service once again. They offered many things—but above all, they offered purpose and adventure.

My advanced degrees and years of overseas business experience made me a strong candidate, though the application process was long and exhaustive. It probed everything—even my reading habits, down to the last five books I had read. That question was easy. I was an avid reader, from devouring the *Hardy Boys* as a kid to passing long Peace Corps nights with books like *The Aztec* and *The Journeyer* by Gary Jennings. The latter, chronicling Marco Polo's epic travels, became a kind of personal guidebook. He walked, rode, and slept his way across the known and unknown world—an ambition I found impossible not to admire.

Training at The Farm to become a certified intelligence operations officer was every bit as demanding as advertised. The first step was to dismantle your ego, then slowly rebuild it into something useful. The process took months, and the Agency had been refining it since the end of World War II. They understood exactly what they were doing. A case officer, above all else, must know his role—and his limits—within the organization. The Farm was beautiful, and the training was exacting. In one exercise, my recruitment target happened to love fishing and owned a small boat. After a few casual restaurant meetings designed to build trust, we took his boat out on the pond. He was an instructor acting as a role player. He knew exactly what was coming: the recruitment pitch—the moment when an intelligence officer formally asks a target to provide information of intelligence value and makes clear that the relationship will be clandestine. It is not a conversation to be rushed. We cast our lines and exchanged small talk. Each time I drew a breath to begin, he shushed me and reeled in his line with exaggerated care, as if he had hooked the Loch Ness Monster. The message was deliberate: timing matters, patience matters, and ego is the enemy. After fifteen minutes of calculated frustration, he finally gave up on Nessie and rowed us back to shore. I very much wanted to drown him. Instead, I swallowed my pride, waited for the right moment, and delivered the pitch on land.

The CIA is an agency of the Executive Branch and is not autonomous; it answers to the administration in power. Its budget and priorities rise and fall with each president's global policies, political agendas, and personnel decisions. Over multiple administrations, I watched operations, resources, and assets expand or contract accordingly.

John C. Maxwell defines leadership simply: *a leader knows the way, goes the way, and shows the way.* I was privileged to stand on the shoulders of giants while leading teams at the CIA, working to make the world safer. Serving my country—working abroad, living in foreign cultures, and defending the Constitution—was a profound honor. It came at a cost, but it also afforded my family and me the rare opportunity to see parts of the world few ever will. I hope I have taken you along on that journey—and, more importantly, inspired you to seek one of your own.

About the Author

Jeffrey Sanow is a highly respected expert in global intelligence, risk management, and strategic leadership, with over 35 years of experience across international operations, security, and executive training. As a former Senior Intelligence Officer in the CIA's National Clandestine Service, Jeffrey played a critical role in high-stakes missions worldwide, focusing on counterproliferation, embassy security, and intelligence operations. As a Senior Intelligence Officer (SIS-1), Jeffrey led operations focusing on weapons of mass destruction, counterintelligence, and high-risk international missions. He also served as a Chief of Station, managing intelligence operations across multiple regions, including South Asia, Southeast Asia, the Middle East, and the eastern Mediterranean. He demonstrated strong cross-cultural intelligence and leadership, working extensively in international operations and managing assets and teams across diverse geopolitical landscapes.

Post-CIA, Jeffrey transitioned into defense contracting, leadership consulting, and corporate training. He has advised elite military units, worked in high-risk international environments, and served as a strategic consultant for businesses aiming to enhance risk management, leadership resilience, and crisis preparedness. Jeffrey served as a U.S. Army Intelligence Advisor, providing pre-combat deployment training and strategic guidance to active-duty intelligence units. He worked as an instructor for Special Operations Forces (SOF) and trained elite military units in tradecraft and operational strategies for missions in Iraq and Afghanistan. As General Manager of Uganda's third-largest security firm, he led high-level security operations, risk management protocols, and the development of organizational strategy.

As a Keynote Speaker & Leadership Coach, Jeffrey trains corporate leaders, security professionals, and military personnel on intelligence-driven leadership and risk assessment. Jeffrey also serves as Senior Special Investigator at Nelson Taplin Goldwater and leads executive protection initiatives, fraud detection, and investigative security consulting.

PH: 863-513-2208
PI # C1800498
Director, Cyber Security, Protection & Investigations,
NTG Consultants

Kymberly "Yeawah" Helwig

CHAPTER FOUR

THE DOORWAY

My extraordinary dream was safety.

At sixteen, I did not know that.

When I reached the door of my parents' apartment, I knocked.

Something inside me felt wrong, and it wasn't just the nausea.

They opened the door, and I saw it on their faces. They already knew.

My father looked at me and said, "What are you doing here? Didn't we tell you that if you got pregnant, you couldn't live here anymore?"

I remembered. I could not stop thinking about it all day.

Earlier that afternoon, my guidance counselor asked why I was crying. I told her I could not tell my parents. They would put me out if they found out. She said, "That's just something parents say. They love you. They wouldn't do that."

She obviously did not believe me. She went behind my back and called them anyway.

It was September 1989. That was the last day I attended that alternative school.

Now I stood in the doorway as my parents handed me two large black garbage bags filled with my clothes.

This event was not the first time I had felt unsafe or discarded in my family. It was the last time I would feel that way and still be able to call that apartment home.

I was sixteen years old, six weeks pregnant, and standing on the streets of Brooklyn, New York, with nowhere to go.

In tears, feeling nauseous, and filled with anxiety, I crossed the street and turned the corner to a friend's house. I knew I could not stay there, but I hoped I could leave my bags. While I was there, I called my boyfriend, the father of my child. I could not stay with him either. That is a story for another chapter.

He did join me that night. We rode the train together until morning, so that I could get some sleep.

The lesson I had been learning throughout my childhood was stamped into my mind that day. Love was conditional. Parents did not have to love you. And if your parents did not love you, no one else would either.

That belief did not arrive as a thought. It accumulated in my body, and it kept score. It shaped how I stood, how I spoke, and what I expected from people. It taught me not to ask for too much. To stay quiet when I was hurt. It taught me to accept what was offered, even when it was barely enough.

I did not have the language for any of this at sixteen. I only knew that the people who were supposed to protect me had chosen not to. An imprint was made on my heart and mind that day, one that screamed, "What you call home can disappear without warning, and any semblance of safety could be revoked without remorse."

After that night, I moved through the world expecting abandonment.

I learned to scan rooms for exits, not get too comfortable, and measure my worth by how useful I could be to others. I believed that love had to be earned and could be snatched away at any moment.

From that point forward, I attracted people and circumstances that confirmed my beliefs. I found myself in relationships where I had to prove my value. I stayed where I was not fully wanted. I tolerated instability and confusion because they felt familiar. When people pulled away, it made sense to me. When love came with conditions, I accepted them.

I did not question the pattern. I thought it was normal. I thought this was what love looked like.

Being put out of my home did not only take away a place to sleep. It took away my sense of belonging. It fractured my trust in authority, in adults, and in systems that claimed to exist for protection. I shared my truth with someone who was supposed to help me, and I ended up paying for it. That lesson stayed with me for years.

I learned to rely on myself too early. To survive without being seen. To keep moving, even when I was exhausted. I learned how to disappear inside my own life.

Pregnancy at sixteen had already placed me outside of what people considered acceptable. Being rejected by my parents sealed my sense of feeling ostracized. I felt marked, different, and alone in ways that I could not express in words.

I did not think about dreams then. I thought about getting through the next day, where I would sleep, and how to stay safe. I thought about how to keep going without asking anyone for help.

What I did not know at the time was that this moment would shape nearly every relationship that followed. The belief that love was conditional became the lens through which I saw myself and the world. It influenced my choices, my silence, and my willingness to settle.

That belief stayed with me far longer than the night I rode the train. It followed me into adulthood. It followed me into love. It followed me into motherhood. It took years before I began to question whether it was true.

At sixteen, all I knew was this. I had been put out. I had survived. And survival, at that point, felt like the only dream available to me.

Eventually, my time of couch-hopping came to an end. I found myself in a group home for young mothers. It was the first place where my baby and I had beds of our own, even if they were not truly ours.

The group home taught me structure. I learned how to be a mother to my daughter. I learned how to wake up on a schedule, complete chores, and follow rules. I learned how to share space with other girls I did not know, all of us carrying our own stories and losses.

I tried to get along with everyone. I stayed polite. I kept my head down. Still, I always felt like an outcast. I carried the quiet belief that someone did not like me, even when no one said so. That feeling followed me from room to room. So, I stayed to myself as much as I could. Solitude felt safer than rejection.

During that time, I worked to earn my GED. Education was the only thing that I felt I had control over. It gave me a sense of movement, even when the rest of my life felt stalled. When I turned 18, I asked to be allowed to get my own place. I believed independence would fix the hurt.

I moved into an apartment in Crown Heights, Brooklyn. I thought I had arrived. I had keys. I had my own door. I had my daughter with me. I believed that having a place meant I was finally safe.

Life became harder instead.

Shortly after I moved into my own place, my daughter's father went to prison. He had not been much help financially, but his absence still landed heavily. When he was gone, the world felt quieter and colder. I felt alone in a way I had not allowed myself to feel before.

I was raising a daughter on my own, and I did not know what I was doing. I had no blueprint and no safety net. I had no one telling me I was doing enough or doing it right.

I carried the responsibility of another life without any guidance. I made decisions without support. I learned to hold fear and determination in the same breath. Some days, I felt strong. Other days, I felt utterly lost.

Loneliness became a constant presence. It sat with me in the apartment at night. It followed me during the day. I wanted someone to see me, to choose me, to stay.

For a long time afterward, I was promiscuous. I did not call it that back then; I thought I was trying to connect, seeking someone to care about me and hoping that person would stay. I desperately yearned for someone to love and choose me, even if only for a moment.

Each encounter was a quiet hope that this one was "the one."

Instead, the pattern repeated. I gave access to people who could not provide stability and would not commit. I offered my body when what I wanted was reassurance. I continued to accept physical closeness without commitment because it felt better than being alone.

I tried to fill an old wound with temporary closeness. Looking back, I can see how clearly the belief followed me. Love was conditional. Love was fleeting. Love had to be earned.

I did not yet know how to interrupt that belief. I only knew how to survive inside it. Survival meant adapting. Survival meant enduring. Survival meant learning how to keep going, even when the cost was high.

At that stage of my life, stability still felt out of reach. I was no longer homeless, but I was not yet grounded. I had a roof, but I did not yet have a sense of home.

That would take time.

What finally began to change things was not hope; it was a desire to give my daughter a better life.

Living in Crown Heights in 1991 was hard. The neighborhood felt tense and unforgiving. I remember watching my daughter sitting at the window, looking outside. She wanted to go out and play. I did not want her out there. I remember thinking there had to be something better than this.

I did not know what that "better" was. I only knew that the life I was living felt like a dead end. I was going nowhere fast, and my daughter was coming with me.

I do not remember precisely how the idea came to me, but one day I decided to join the military. Maybe it was the photographs I had seen of my father and my uncle in uniform. Perhaps the idea had been planted long before I noticed it. I only know that, at the time, it felt like the only way out of the cycle I was in.

So, I went to the recruiting station in downtown Brooklyn.

That was where I first learned about college.

The recruiter told me I would be better off getting some college credits before joining, since I had a GED. No one had ever suggested college to me before. It felt unfamiliar and intimidating, but I listened.

I enrolled at Medgar Evers College and took my first semester. College was more complicated than I expected. I was afraid most of the time. I did not do well that semester. I felt overwhelmed and unsure of myself, and eventually, I transferred to Borough of Manhattan Community College.

I did a little better there. I kept going. I earned the credits I needed. When I had enough, I returned to the recruiting station. I took the ASVAB. Not long after that, I signed on the dotted line.

There was a catch.

You cannot join the military as a single parent with custody of a child. I had to leave my daughter behind for a while. I had to give temporary custody to a family member.

That decision broke something open inside me.

My friends did not understand. Some thought I was abandoning my child. Some thought I was a bad mother for choosing to leave her, even temporarily. Their judgment cut deeply, but I could not see another way.

I was not leaving her because I did not love her. I

was leaving because I loved her. I could not find another path that offered stability, education, and a chance at something different.

It was the hardest decision I had made up to that point. It went against everything I wanted emotionally, but it was the first time I had chosen long-term safety over immediate comfort.

I carried guilt with me every day. I carried fear. I carried doubt. But I also carried a quiet resolve.

I told myself that this separation was temporary. That this sacrifice had meaning. I just had to endure this part, and I could give my daughter more than survival. My decision did not fix everything. It did not erase my past. But it did give me hope for a better future for my child and me.

My time with the military brought its own layers of change, problems, and moments of joy. It did not save me. It reshaped me.

The military gave me structure and direction, but it also exposed me to new harm. During my service, I experienced military sexual trauma, and with it, depression settled in quietly and stayed. Some days, it showed up as exhaustion. Other days, it showed up as numbness or isolation. I learned how to function while feeling heavy inside.

Six months after joining the service, I got married. With my new husband, I inherited a daughter. After two years, two more children followed. I became a mother again and again, each time carrying more responsibility, more love, and a growing sense of pressure I did not have the capacity to name.

Over the years, I continued taking college classes, here and there, and kept moving forward on paper. From the outside, it looked like progress. But on the inside, I was tormented by sadness, fear, and the old beliefs that whispered, "Struggle and neglect are normal. Brace for it."

While raising my children, I manifested my trauma onto them. Not intentionally, but depression made patience harder. It shortened my emotional reach. I did the best I could with what I understood at the time, but I can see now where harm traveled forward.

The one thing that remained steady while raising my children was my desire to do better. Even in depression, that desire never left. Sometimes I could not act on it. Many times, I fell short, but it stayed present.

That desire showed up in small, quiet ways. I read books that spoke about healing and becoming a better person. I went to therapy when I could. I attended workshops and did the affirmations. I tried many churches. These choices did not cure me, but they kept me connected to the idea that change was possible.

For a long time, it felt like none of it was working. Depression made progress feel nonexistent. I was still tired and still repeating patterns I wanted to break. I would go into my closet and cry and pray to be better. I thought growth would feel clearer and faster than it did.

It took years for me to understand that something was building, even when I could not feel it. Spirituality, reading, affirmations, and therapy mattered. Each effort added a layer of awareness and strength.

My marriage lasted nineteen years. I stayed longer than I should have, partly because depression blurred my sense of choice. It made endurance feel necessary, and leaving impossible. I believed that wanting things to work was the same as making them work.

Eventually, my marriage ended in divorce. It was painful, but it was honest. It marked the end of a long season of surviving through obligation and dysfunction.

Looking back, I can see that my years with the military and in my marriage were not a detour. They were an extended classroom that revealed my limits and my endurance. They revealed to me the cost of unaddressed trauma.

That accumulation of painful experiences and the self-work make up who I am today. Someone aware, still learning, and committed to doing better than those who came before me. Someone accountable. Someone I can be proud of.

Eventually, all that work began to change how I related to myself and to my children. I reached a point where I could no longer avoid the truth. Trauma does not just stop because we want it to; it gets passed down generationally until someone says, "No more." Just like my parents, I also caused harm to my children. Love required that I be held accountable and take responsibility for what I had done.

So, I did.

I listened to my adult children without defending myself. I named my mistakes without explanation or excuse. I worked on repairing what could be repaired, and I stayed present when repair felt slow or incomplete. Accountability became part of my healing. It grounded me in reality and taught me that love could exist alongside truth.

Around the same time, I found love and safety in my relationship with my life partner. This relationship did not require me to prove my worth or earn my place. It offered steadiness, respect, and care. Inside that safety, I could finally rest, cry, and share my truth.

It was in our relationship that more profound healing began.

I started speaking to the child inside me, the sixteen-year-old who stood on a Brooklyn sidewalk with two garbage bags and nowhere to go. I told her what she had never been told: "You are safe, and love does not mean you will be put out."

That inner work mattered as much as anything else I had done.

After more than thirty years of working toward a college degree, I graduated from Columbia University with a bachelor's degree in psychology. An Ivy League degree was never part of my original plan. It became possible only after I stopped believing that I was not meant for stability, achievement, or belonging.

The degree did not erase the past. It did not fix everything. But it stood as proof that the girl who was once put out of her family's home, an extraordinary trauma, had built a life that could hold her.

For a long time, I thought extraordinary dreams were about success, recognition, or arrival.

Mine was simpler.

My extraordinary dream was safety.

Safety in my body.

Safety in my relationships.

Safety in telling the truth.

And I am living inside that dream now.

About the Author

Kymberly "Yeawah" Helwig is a Certified Peer Support Specialist, United States Army veteran, and 2026 graduate of Columbia University, where she earned her BA in Psychology. She is the mother of four adult children and writes about resilience, identity, and generational healing. A survivor of childhood sexual abuse and military sexual trauma, she transforms lived experience into scholarship, advocacy, and community leadership.

Kymberly coined the terms Afrilineal and Afrigenic to distinguish lineage from phenotype and to honor the descendants of enslaved Africans across the diaspora. Afrilineal names direct descent from enslaved Africans in the Americas. Afrigenic describes visible African traits without assuming lineage. Through this language, she challenges racial classification and restores dignity to inherited identity.

Through DNA testing, she traced her ancestry to the Mende people of Sierra Leone. In 2021, she traveled to Sierra Leone, obtained citizenship, and was adopted into a Mende family, receiving the name Yeawah Siawo Sharif. This reconnection to lineage deepened her commitment to Afrilineal restoration and generational healing.

Her work centers on strengthening families, redefining identity after trauma, and building peer-led spaces for relational health.

LinkedIn: https://www.linkedin.com/in/kymberly-helwig-413b15126
IG: www.instagram.com/salonebigmum21
Email: yeyekym21@gmail.com

Cesar R. Espino, MBA

CHAPTER FIVE

UNBREAKABLE
RISING BEYOND EVERY OBSTACLE

I didn't come from comfort. I came from conditions that most people would look at and quietly decide, "the odds are against him." But what I've learned through every season of my life is this: your circumstances may shape your starting point, but they do not determine your destination.

When I look back, I don't see a perfect path. I see resistance. I see pressure. I see moments that could have broken me. And in every one of those moments, there was a decision to make—stay down, or rise.

I chose to rise.

When I reflect on my life, one truth stands out clearly: quitting was never part of the plan. The only reason I am where I am today is because I chose—again and again—to keep going, even when everything around me suggested I shouldn't. I want to share my story not just to tell you where I've been, but to show you what's possible when you refuse to give up.

I was born in Mexico City into a family that had very little financially, but more strength than I could understand at the time. I didn't grow up with my biological father (never met him and to this day I do not even know his name), and for many, that becomes a defining limitation. But my life was shaped by something more powerful—resilience, sacrifice, and love from my mother and grandmother.

Our home was not what most people would consider livable. It was a small space, a single room—barely 200 square feet built from plywood and sheet metal, with no electricity, no running water, and no real flooring—just dirt beneath our feet. Four of us shared that space. It wasn't comfortable, but it was ours.

And even in those conditions, something was being developed inside of me—something far greater than comfort: perspective.

Because when you grow up without much, you learn early to appreciate everything. You learn that nothing is guaranteed. And you learn that if anything is going to change, it starts with you.

At around four years old, my life shifted dramatically. My mother made a decision that would impact me for years to come—she left for the United States in search of a better life for our family.

She didn't leave out of desire.

She left out of necessity.

And just like that, I began a new chapter of my life—one without my mother physically present.

For six years, I grew up being raised by my grandmother, alongside my older brother. During those years, I didn't experience a traditional childhood. Instead, I stepped into responsibility early.

I began working at a very young age.

I sold food at the *"tianguis"* an open-air market—donuts, bread, taquitos, whatever we could manage. I learned what it meant to earn, to contribute, and to survive.

There were days when food was scarce.

There were times when the only thing available to eat was a tortilla with grains of salt, which I like to call the Mexican Specialty Dish (it's not really, I've just called it that way, hahaha). And to this day, I still enjoy it as it is really good. And while that might sound difficult, it taught me something powerful: you can endure more than you think you can.

There were moments when I would find small leftovers—things others discarded—and I would see them as opportunity, not shame. Because hunger doesn't care about pride—it teaches humility. One of my favorites things to find, specially when I will go to school, was a *"Duvalin"* in the trash or on the floor that still had some candy on it. I would pick it up and eat it (Duvalin is a popular Mexican candy known for its creamy texture and unique flavors, typically offered in combinations like Hazelnut and Vanilla or Hazelnut and Strawberry).

Looking back now, I realize those were not just hard times… they were training grounds.

They built my work ethic.

They built my hunger.

They built my resilience.

Eventually, my mom came back to Mexico and this time she came to take us (my grandma, older brother, and I) to the United States, and start a new life with her and the man she met in the states, my stepdad, who I see and recognized as my dad, because he fulfilled that void in my life of that male figure and has been a true dad, when he did not have to. The journey to the United States was no sunshine and rainbows, as a matter of fact it was challenging, almost two weeks challenging as I did not come here legally and had to crossed the border in really difficult conditions (that story will take more than just a chapter for me to described the suffering and things my family and I went through, just to come to the states). But arriving here didn't mean life suddenly became easy. In many ways, it became more challenging.

New country.

New culture.

New language.

And once again, I felt like I didn't belong, I had no friends, was bullied, and to an extend I was living with a man who I really did not know and my mom who to an extend at that time was a stranger to me given, she was absent from my life for so many years. Now, looking back I fully understand that her leaving me was not easy at all, and it needed to happen to have a better chance and opportunity in life, and for that I am grateful.

Being new to the states, I struggled to communicate. I struggled to connect. I struggled to understand where I fit. That frustration sometimes turned into anger, and that anger showed up in ways I wasn't proud of—fights, resistance, and poor reactions.

But something inside me refused to stay there.

At some point, I made a shift.

I stopped asking, "Why is this happening to me?" and started asking, "What can I do with this?"

That one shift changed everything.

Instead of resisting the situation, I began to embrace the process of growth. I focused on learning the language. I focused on improving in school. I focused on becoming better.

And slowly, I began to transform.

I went from feeling invisible… to being recognized.

By middle school, I was achieving academically. I was earning respect. And I was given the opportunity to stand in front of my classmates and deliver a graduation speech.

We Choose Our Way

Good morning, everyone! Today is a very special day for all of us. We are the first eighth-grade class graduating from Mt. Vernon Middle School. I feel so honored today to represent my friends and peers on this occasion.

First of all, I would like to say something to our faculty at Mt. Vernon. On behalf of the eighth-grade class, I would like to thank you for all the encouragement you have given us over the last two years.

Next, on behalf of the eighth grade, I would like to say something to our parents. You have always been there when we have needed you. You made sure that we got to school and got there on time. Also, you strongly encouraged us to do our homework when we didn't want to. This has given us a discipline that will help us in the future.

And finally, I would like to say something to the graduates today. We have been here at Mt. Vernon Middle School for two years, and it is now time to go on. We have finished our experience here, and it is now time to face new ones. Many of us are going to choose a way that will get us into college. We would choose a good education and a good life. Others, unfortunately, will choose the way of gangs and drugs. For them, the future looks dark. My challenge to all of us today is to choose the way of education. In this choice, we will not only improve our own lives, but we will also set an example for our community.

As I close, again, I would like to say, we have much to be thankful for. We have many memories to take with us as we leave Mt. Vernon, and again, on behalf of the eighth grade, I thank our principal, teachers, families, and honored guests for all they have done to help us see our dream come true.

That moment meant more than just words.

It was proof.

Proof that where you start does not define where you can go.

Proof that growth is possible.

Proof that change happens when you commit to it.

But life continued to test me.

In high school, I made a decision that would impact the rest of my life.

I became a father at a very young age; to be exact my girlfriend at the time and I got pregnant at the age of 15, and we had our baby girl at the age of 16. This was not easy at all; I was a kid having a kid.

Now, let's be honest—that kind of responsibility at that stage of life can break many people. It can derail plans, create fear, and reinforce limitations.

But I made a different choice.

I chose to step up.

I chose to take responsibility.

I chose to grow.

My daughter became my reason, my why.

She became the driving force behind every decision I made moving forward, especially because I did not want my daughter to suffer the same way I did, or yet alone grew up without a father, or have to worry about working at an early age, just like I did, or sometimes not having anything to eat.

Every time I felt like quitting…

Every time I felt overwhelmed…

Every time I questioned whether I could handle it…

I would remind myself: this is bigger than you.

That belief gave me strength I didn't know I had.

And while I wasn't perfect—and still am not—I made a commitment to do whatever it took to give her a better life than the one I had experienced growing up.

That commitment changed everything.

But the journey didn't suddenly become smooth.

I faced more adversity.

I made mistakes.

I experienced setbacks—legal trouble, job loss, uncertainty, and moments of deep doubt.

There were nights filled with frustration. Nights where the future felt unclear. Nights where giving up felt like the easiest option.

But I didn't.

Because I had purpose.

And purpose will push you when motivation disappears.

I kept going.

I kept learning.

I kept growing.

And over time, I began to understand something that many people overlook:

Your life is a reflection of the decisions you make consistently—not occasionally.

And if a decision isn't working, you have the power to change it.

"Our quality of future is dependent on the decisions and choices we make today"
~Cesar R. Espino

"The choices and decisions we make today, will impact the quality of life we have tomorrow."
~Cesar R. Espino

You are not stuck.

You are not limited.

You are not defined by your past.

You are shaped by your willingness to adapt.

Over the years, I began to develop habits that strengthened my mindset and helped me stay focused.

I became intentional with my language.

I removed words that created limitations and replaced them with words that created possibility.

I stopped saying "I can't" and started asking "How can I?"

I stopped seeing problems and started seeing challenges.

I stopped hoping… and started believing and having

faith.

Because words ***do* matter.**

The way you speak becomes the way you think.

Here are some words that you want to remove and or substitute from your vocabulary:

- Removed the word **Try** – either do it or don't – false action, it also already implies a failure action (no physical state of try)
- Do not use the word **Can't** – recognize you don't know how to (so learn how to do it), or don't want to (not because you can't).
- Removed the word(s) **But/However** – negates everything before it, replaced by "and."
- Remove the word **No** – Replace with "yes and."
- Remove the words **Problem** or **Issue** – replace them with "challenge." A problem or Issue has a negative connotation, and by default, we as humans do not want to deal with that. On the contrary, a challenge is a positive thing. As human beings, we want to be challenged because we want to solve that challenge and find a solution.
- Get rid of **Hope** – instead, be certain and use the word "know" or "faith."
- Get rid of the word **If** – instead use "when." E.g., If I win the lottery, I will buy myself a house – instead of "when" I win the lottery, I will buy myself a house.
- Get rid of the word **Why** – instead substitute it with "what" or "how."
- Get rid of a **resolution**, or **goals**, instead set up specific "plans" and "targets."
- Instead of **worried** – replace with "wonder" (positive wondering).

- Instead of **Doubt** – replace with "determination" (be certain, be determined).
- When stress or the thought of **stress** – just surrender, review, and analyze the situation.

Remember that the way you think becomes the way you act, as what you focus on it will expand, *focus on good outcomes.*

I also became intentional about my environment.

I evaluated the people around me.

Were they pushing me forward… or holding me back?

Because who you spend time with will either expand your vision or shrink it.

I chose growth.

I sought mentorship.

I surrounded myself with people who were building, learning, and striving for more.

I joined communities that encouraged progress.

I created accountability in my life.

I began journaling—writing down my thoughts, my goals, and my plans.

And something powerful happens when you write things down: you create clarity.

You begin to see direction.

You begin to take control.

I also implemented daily affirmations.

Create your own, and not just read in your mind or a quiet voice. Say it out loud, proud and loud. Feel the emotion and imagine the action. Here are some of my own I created a while back (I now have this on my daily journal on my first page. I go on to them, and then I journal or write down the things I must get done today).

I declared who I was becoming—even before I fully saw it.

- I am disciplined
- I am capable
- I am unstoppable
- I am entrepreneurial
- I am successful
- I am healthy
- I am spiritually sound and focused
- I am surrounded by love
- I am rich
- I am wanted
- I am loved
- I am happy
- I am blessed
- I am at peace with everything and everyone
- I attract new clients every day
- I am attractive
- I wake up happy and excited every single day
- I have a lot of money
- I am helpful
- I am a great partner
- I am wealthy
- I am abundant
- I am beautiful
- I am committed
- I am generous and helpful
- I am kind and loving
- I am confident
- I am strong
- I am certain
- I am grateful

- I am deserving of all my dreams
- I love my life
- I am fearless
- I am a millionaire

Because before something becomes your reality… it must first become your belief.

I committed to daily movement.

Not because it was easy—but because it built discipline.

Sometimes it was just a walk.

Sometimes it was listening to something that fueled my mindset.

But every day, I did something to move forward.

And those small actions compounded over time.

That's how transformation happens.

Not in one moment—but in many small moments stacked together.

I also learned to plan.

Not just dream—but plan.

Because dreams without action stay dreams.

But plans create progress.

I wrote down what I needed to do each day, each week.

And every time I completed something, I acknowledged it.

Because progress builds confidence.

And confidence fuels more progress.

Through all of this, I came to understand a powerful truth:

Life will hit you.

It will challenge you.

It will test your patience, your strength, and your belief.

But it's not about avoiding those moments.

It's about who you become through them.

Because resilience is not built in comfort—it's built in adversity.

Today, I'm still growing.

Still learning.

Still evolving.

I haven't arrived—and that's the point.

Because growth is not a destination.

It's a commitment.

A daily decision to become better than you were yesterday.

So wherever you are right now…

Whether you're struggling…

Whether you're uncertain…

Whether you feel behind…

Understand this:

> You are not finished.
>
> Your story is still being written.
>
> And you have more control than you think.
>
> You can rise.
>
> You can rebuild.
>
> You can create something greater.
>
> But it starts with a decision.
>
> A decision to stop making excuses.
>
> A decision to take ownership.
>
> A decision to move forward—no matter how small the step.
>
> Because small steps still move you forward.
>
> And forward is all you need.
>
> You don't need perfect conditions.
>
> You don't need approval.
>
> You don't need everything figured out.
>
> You just need to start.

And keep going.

Because the version of you that you're meant to become…
Is waiting on the other side of your commitment.
Stay strong.
Stay focused.
And become unbreakable.

Last and not least, get into the habit of reading books that are going to move you forward in life. Read educational or self-help books, like *You Can Overcome Anything! Even When the World Says "No", or any of the You Can Overcome Anything! Book series, The Miracle Morning, Think and Growth Rich, The Cashflow Quadrant, The Compound Effect,* just to name a few.

"Let me tell you something you already know. The world isn't all sunshine and rainbows. It's a very mean and nasty place, and I don't care how tough you are. It will beat you to your knees and keep you there permanently if you let it. You, me, or nobody will hit as hard as life. But it isn't about how hard you hit. It's about how hard you can get hit and keep moving ahead. How much you can take and keep moving ahead. That's how winning is done!
~ Sylvester Stallone

You can learn more about my life, the challenges, and the changes I had to make to become who I am and where I am now. The journey is not yet over. To get the full, pick up your copy of *You Can Overcome Anything! Even When the World Says "NO".*

"I am not perfect, and I've been handed down so many lessons, except I've learned, I've grown, and the rest of my life I will live becoming the best version of me each day." ~ Cesar R. Espino

About the Author

Cesar R. Espino is the creator of You Can Overcome Anything! Podcast Show, You Can Overcome Anything Book Series, a real estate investor, mindset coach, business consultant, and multiple #1 best-selling international book author. His passion and highest intention are to empower, inspire, and motivate others to reach their full potential. Cesar offers a variety of tools and services to help people improve their current situation. He is creating opportunities for people to have a chance at life regardless of their background and current situation. He believes that while you have no say in which family you were born into, you have the choice to make your destiny with perseverance, growth, faith, and belief in yourself to become the best version of yourself, regardless of the odds or the society into which you were born.

Website: www.CesarRespino.com
www.linktree.com/espinoc
Podcast: https://podcasts.apple.com/us/podcast/you-can-overcome-anything-podcast-show/id1497917624?uo=4

Symone Fairchild

CHAPTER SIX

I. AM. PRESENCE.

I. AM. PRESENCE. I AM PRESENCE. This is what you come to realize you have become... CORRECTION... this is what you come to realize you have ALWAYS BEEN once you have braved the journey to your greatest self. Once you have healed so much that your nervous system has assumed its origin state. In other words, you no longer have any triggers or trauma wounds. You can exist in this world and this world NO LONGER TRIGGERS YOU. This is what *Extraordinary Trauma To Extraordinary Dreams* looks like. This is where I am, and this is how I got here.

Whenever I am asked about my journey, and now,

whenever I think about it in retrospect, I always work backward from now as my starting point. I have come to understand that this is the case because this is how I healed. I had to start from where I was. And, yes, I was scared, but I was so much more determined than I was scared. I knew that my circumstances were not my destiny…not then, not ever. I knew that trauma and pain and fear and the state of things at the time were not who I was and not what I was meant for. So, I strapped up my proverbial boots and got to walkin'... on fire!

Before being the unobstructed vessel of **I AM PRESENCE** that I am now. Prior to my mind (ego) surrendering and aligning with my SPIRIT, soul, heart, and body. Before enlightenment, I was on the unyielding journey of what I knew was Thriving. I have come to understand that every being that has ever lived, is living now, and will ever live, is meant to thrive. And, thriving is leaning into one's SPIRIT, soul, heart, mind, and body, every day, and to the point where one's body (vessel) becomes unobstructed, allowing I AM PRESENCE to exist completely. It's the handing-over-of-the-wheel, so to speak. The most amazing things start to happen in one's reality once this change starts to occur: DIVINE wisdom begins to funnel through your mind, truth (and lies) start to jump out in conversations as if words jumping off of a page, one inherently knows who and who not to be around, what and what not to do, what they are meant for.

The way I am supposed to go, the things I am supposed to do are lit up in me as if the way is no longer unknown. In fact, what my journey has taught me is to "see in the dark." You know how we have been taught to see the unknown as darkness? No sound. No light. No nothing. It's not that the unknown is no longer unknown; it's that I know how to read it all. I know how to read it all because I am completely aware of who I am (I AM). I have done the internal work and built the internal structure, and when that work is done, all will be revealed to you. Why? Because your vessel, your nervous system especially, can handle not only the information but, most importantly, the frequency...the vibration. But, before I go down that rabbit hole, let's continue to walk back along my journey.

Let's jump into the question you are probably asking: What happened that sparked this inner work? Well, before I understood that I was on a quest for Thrivership, I was a survivor. I was still a survivor, knocking my head up against the same wall over and over again, not understanding how to get over it, under it, around it, or even through it. I just couldn't get past survivorship. It was another point where I got stuck...another point where, it turns out, I had to BE STILL. Be still, watch, listen, especially within but also match what the Universe was sending me in my environment (without). I didn't understand this yet, not until I was circling enlightenment. I didn't understand yet that the Universe would send me Mirrors. These were people (other vessels) that matched my frequency and had messages for me, if you will. They showed up to "mirror" parts of me that I was missing, parts of my present experience that I was missing, deliver tools or resources that I needed to uplevel, be a support, tell me to slow down, or just remind me of who I AM, etc. The survivor was still there, but I knew what I was headed for. I just didn't know how to get there.

Why was I a survivor, and what did I have to survive? Well, at first, I was a *victim* of domestic abuse. I experienced physical, emotional/psychological, sexual, financial, spiritual, legal, tech abuse, and stalking. My son and I are just my son and I for this reason. It was absolutely awful and wrecked my nervous system. Then, as I grew and healed, I became a *survivor* of domestic abuse. I spent most of my 9-year journey here. I did so because of the programming within society that so strongly influences us to be a survivor, especially if you are a woman. "I'm A Survivor," right? The Beyoncé song. The problem with that is when you are a survivor, you have to have survived something. Your story is still rooted in some trauma. And, if your mouth still speaks a story rooted in trauma, your mind still operates from a reality of trauma, which reflects in one's exterior environment. Again, I knew that wasn't what I was meant for, especially since I am a single mom (of the most awesome boy on the planet!). Being a single mom means there is someone on this planet who relies completely on you. I would never have resided there. My son needed me to be the best I could be. My son needed me to be his example. Plain and simple.

Going back further was my experience in Hollywood. My Divine gift is acting. It is the one thing that I do that doesn't take energy from me. It actually gives me energy…it feeds me. I can spend 16 hours on a set and be absolutely buzzing with energy by the time "wrap" is called. This is because it is creation. I AM a CREATOR. It is my heart and soul-center. It is the symbiotic relationship at my core through which I channel the Divine. I absolutely love it. The only problem is that, as we can all see now, given report after report in the media, the entertainment industry is a very dark place… not because of Hollywood itself, but because of the people who hold the keys to it. In other words, the gatekeepers.

I have had several opportunities to "make it." Still, just about every time an opportunity was presented, at some point in the process, it became clear that for me to walk through that door of opportunity, a sexual relationship was the price. I experienced sexual harassment or sexual assault in quite a few instances. I call it being "Weinstein-ed," and it is EVERYWHERE within the entertainment industry. Most either give in to it in exchange for success and fame. Some quit because of it. To each his own. I, on the other hand, always knew that I would never "sell my soul." NEVER. So, then, what was my choice? Create my own. I come from a family of entrepreneurs. I have that coursing through my veins. I certainly wasn't going to quit. That word, QUIT, is not in my vocabulary. I had to pivot. And pivot I certainly did. HARD. I have created the structure for an entire empire with a production company and library of film and television projects at the center, a non-profit organization benefiting domestic abuse (trauma) victims and survivors, with books and speaking included. The pain of Hollywood has propelled me toward the purpose of providing a safe space for others, and this book is an extraordinary example.

Now, childhood. The earthly seed of it all…not only of the trauma, but in retrospect, the earthly source of what makes it all make sense. I have talked about my journey before, so the whole thing isn't new. I do have to say, though, that it has taken me a few days to actually sit down at the keyboard to type out this part. I have never written about my childhood experiences before, and just thinking about it… brings up some emotions. My heart is beating more quickly. I can feel the tears building in my throat. Writing this, sharing it with you… I am releasing it into the world. I am

RELEASING it. In doing so, I am leaving space for something new to take its place. Just the thought of that alone brings me to tears because there is so much that I have built, internally and externally, so much work that has been done, so much preparation. I can't wait to see what takes its place.

So… here goes. I was raised in a martial arts household. It was our life. Discipline. Discipline. Discipline that, today, I am grateful for being a woman, an entrepreneur, and in the entertainment business. Being raised in this art was highly competitive, constantly. There was no crying, no emotion, no sharing of one's feelings allowed. On the flipside, there was a centeredness and groundedness that were natural elements of the art. There was a sense of protectiveness toward others, an awareness of one's surroundings, and a warrior aspect to things. This is ingrained in my DNA and has been since the age of 3 ½.

Now, at 9 years old, I had to be transferred to a new elementary school because the 5th-grade teacher was, to put it mildly, less than ideal for me. The reason this occurrence stands out in my journey is that it also meant my parents no longer needed a babysitter for my sister and me, since the new school we would be going to was so close to our home that we could walk to and from school. At that point, my sister and I were removed from an environment in which I had been molested for years. Thinking back, I remember everything about it. It's as clear as day, except for the bedroom of their 18-year-old son. It was tucked down at the very end of the upstairs hallway, and we were banned from going down there. We never did. I never would have ventured down there because if I did, I knew I would be trapped. I remember every aspect of the basement because that is where it always happened. Strangely, it was always so bright and cozy and clean down there, despite the horrors that were occurring in the space. Every time it happened, I would run upstairs to my sister because I knew, even at that young age, that if it were happening to me, it wasn't happening to her. I was her protector…no matter what. No matter where we were or who was around, she would always be protected. This wasn't the case for me, though. I tried and tried to share what was going on, but no one ever listened or did anything about it. There was never any justice, and I carried that and other aspects of my childhood that I will share at a later date into my teens, causing years of suicidal tendencies and what I later came to understand as high-functioning depression, anxiety, and C-PTSD.

Sounds awful, right? Yes, it was, and it haunted me for quite a while. But what I have come to understand in the last 9 years of my life is that this childhood experience was the first of many in which the LIGHT within me, the Divine power within me, took over. It shone through and, without knowing it at the time, I leaned into it. I could have easily taken a turn and chosen a very dark path. But I didn't. I was never meant to. I was always a very quiet child, so I naturally leaned more into the quiet, safe space within. I leaned more into writing and into things I enjoyed, like animals and cheerleading (which I was actually fantastic at). This is where my love of film and television began. I watched everything I could get my hands on: beauty pageants, nature shows, and action movies. No horror, though… didn't care for that at all. I had enough of that going on in real life. I loved it for the lessons, the messages, the TRUTH in the stories, and the programming I was watching. What I was naturally resonating with was the silver lining…the Divine Truth that was within me, I was finding it in what I was watching. I leaned heavily into school and wanted to become a veterinarian or a model. This carried on for quite a while. I have been goal-oriented ever since.

Fast-forward to the start of my spiritual journey. A 9-year process ignited by my domestic abuse experience (which I will share in detail at a later date). During that relationship, I became very drawn to God. I leaned into church, church groups, Bible studies, everything. I remember sitting down to do Bible study assignments, not realizing I had been at it for hours. I absolutely loved it and chased after God like my hair was on fire. That was the beginning… the beginning of the enlightenment's journey. It was also the beginning of the understanding of the Universe through understanding myself. I dove down the rabbit hole initially to understand my abuser.

Further down, I began to understand that I was rediscovering myself. I was so driven to keep going because I was getting external Divine verification "out of nowhere" that somehow aligned with a KNOWING I had within me that kept growing and growing. The more I leaned into it, the more I was shown, the more I grew, the more I expanded, the more I upleveled. Sometimes, it scared the living shit out of me because I would plateau and couldn't keep moving, no matter what I did. In those instances, I learned to sit still. For 9 years, I kept at it day after day after day. I had to. Initially, I had to for my son. I came to understand, after a while, that I had to do it for MYSELF. I went through this Divine process at the very same time as I was healing from domestic abuse and giving everything I had to establishing a solid foundation for my son and me alone. I can't possibly explain how difficult it was, but at the same time, how absolutely invigorating it was. Going through these two journeys simultaneously was a blessing because the Divine rediscovery of myself gave me an ever-expanding perspective on what I was going through, from what I call "boots on the ground" and from the bird's eye perspective. It also gave me the strength to start seeing Divine Truth in everything and to filter out the noise. At a certain point, I just KNEW it was time to set boundaries. Because I was doing so much internal work, I could hear and feel the gentle nudges my body was giving me about where a boundary belonged. It eventually became very easy to tell when someone was telling me the truth and when they weren't.

During this process, my mission on the planet became clearer and clearer. All along the way, I built it and molded it and, at times, released what no longer belonged to it or to me. There is so much more I can say about my spiritual journey, but unfortunately, I don't have enough space to do so here. But, I will give you the end point: I have done so much inner work that it has led to enlightenment, then the surrendering of my mind, which led to understanding that I am the I AM, and then, finally, one day, realizing that I had healed my nervous system not just completely but back to its origin state. I no longer have any triggers or wounds. When this happens, you have a baseline frequency so high that you exist in the world, but you're not of it. And, this state is what every one of us is meant for.

The only thing that is different about me is that I leaned into my tools. And once I got the hang of it, I did so every day. EVERYDAY. And, at 100 mph with fear as rocket fuel in my veins instead of cement boots holding me in a perpetual cycle of trauma. I used my fear instead of letting it control me. Mind over matter. This is superhero stuff I'm talkin' about here, and we all have it. YOU have it. I often hear people say, "How can I change the world? I'm just one person." This is exactly how....by changing you FIRST. Then, the after-effects of healing yourself have an automatic impact on your environment and on the world. Here's a direct example: Remember how I said that I have healed my nervous system back to its origin state? Well, there is a greater meaning to this outside of myself. It also means that I am not passing trauma down to my son. I HAVE HEALED MY BLOODLINE. From my son on down, no further generations will have unknown or unseen generational trauma impacting their development, personalities, or mindset. Do you know how huge that is?! And that's just within my family. My inner healing also changes the energy my body emits into the environment, which, in turn, changes who and what I attract. Again, do you know how huge that is? I am now an unobstructed vessel in which all the high-frequency things, opportunities, relationships that have been waiting around for me to be ready for can now pour in, and the excess can bubble over into whoever and whatever is in my field. I can share and give from overflow, not from depletion, system overload, or people-pleasing. I'm ready. That's superhero stuff! And I just leaned into the tools we all have… the ones you have.

So, fellow superhero, I have one question for you: What color is your cape?

About the Author

Symone Fairchild is a transformational leader, creative visionary, and Master of Northern Shaolin Kung-Fu who turned childhood trauma and survival of domestic abuse into a life of purpose and impact. An actress, writer, director, and executive producer, she is devoted to bringing truth to light through story. Her work centers on helping others rise beyond adversity and reclaim their power. Through this anthology, she continues her mission of transforming pain into purpose and vision into legacy.

www.symonefairchild.com

About the Author

[illegible]

About the Author

Symone Fairchild hails from the Washington, D.C. area and was raised in the discipline and philosophy of martial arts, eventually becoming a Master of Northern Shaolin Kung-Fu. From a young age, she navigated childhood trauma on her own, developing an unshakable resilience and a relentless entrepreneurial spirit. Martial arts was not just training—it was a way of life that forged her tenacity, focus, and unwavering belief in rising after every fall.

Having thrived beyond domestic abuse, Symone came to understand that her survival was not random—it was preparation. Her gifts became clear. Acting allows her to breathe truth and light into the human experience. Writing enables her to articulate what others struggle to say. Directing gives her the power to shape vision into reality. Producing allows her to bring together the exact people and resources required to manifest purpose into form.

At the core of her journey is a deep spiritual alignment with God, The Source of all things, and a devotion to her son—the two anchors of her life. By fully leaning into her inner Light and destined strength, Symone has embraced her calling: to bring Divine Truth to life in the world. Her mission is not only to inspire transformation but to model it—to show humanity what is possible when pain is alchemized into purpose.

With Extraordinary Trauma To Extraordinary Dreams, she invites others to rise alongside her—not despite what they endured, but because of it.

Websites: www.symonefairchild.com
www.dragonentertainmentfilm.com
www.eyeondv.com
Tiktok: https://www.tiktok.com/@symonefairchild?_r=1&_t=ZP-93vfiSFp5iA
IG: https://www.instagram.com/eyeondv
FB: https://www.facebook.com/symone.fairchild.5
YouTube: https://youtube.com/@eyeondv1355?si=U0gIYQo0UD-RcVM_
LinkedIn: https://www.linkedin.com/in/symone-fairchild-30b69515/

www.ingramcontent.com/pod-product-compliance
Lightning Source LLC
LaVergne TN
LVHW010939110826
845149LV00013B/2681

* 9 7 8 1 9 6 0 6 6 5 3 7 9 *